THE NETHERLANDS
WORLD ADVENTURES
BY STEFFI CAVELL-CLARKE

BookLife

©2017
Book Life
King's Lynn
Norfolk PE30 4LS

ISBN: 978-1-78637-127-0

Written by:
Steffi Cavell-Clarke

Edited by:
Charlie Ogden

Designed by:
Matt Rumbelow

A catalogue record for this book
is available from the British Library.

THE NETHERLANDS
WORLD ADVENTURES

CONTENTS

Words in **red** can be found in the glossary on page 24.

WHERE IS THE NETHERLANDS?

The Netherlands is a small country found in the western part of Europe.

THE NETHERLANDS

The capital city of the Netherlands is Amsterdam.

AMSTERDAM, NETHERLANDS

The **population** of the Netherlands is over 16 million.
The main language in the Netherlands is **Dutch**.

WEATHER AND LANDSCAPE

The weather in the Netherlands changes with the seasons. It gets hotter in the summer and cooler in the winter.

The Netherlands is known for its flat landscape and long rivers. The city of Amsterdam has many canals.

CLOTHING

Many different types of **traditional** clothing are still worn in the Netherlands today. Many Dutch women wear long dresses and white hats.

Clogs are a type of footwear. They were traditionally worn by farmers. They are made out of wood and can be worn by men and women.

RELIGION

The **religion** with the most followers in the Netherlands is Christianity. The Christian place of **worship** is a church.

Many people in the Netherlands follow other religions, such as Islam and Hinduism. There are also people who do not follow any religion.

FOOD

The stroopwafel is a popular biscuit in the Netherlands. It is made out of two pieces of waffle and is filled with a sweet sauce.

STROOPWAFEL

Many types of cheese are made in the Netherlands and sent all over the world for people to eat. One of the most famous cheese from the Netherlands is called Edam.

EDAM

AT SCHOOL

Children in the Netherlands start school at the age of five. At school, young children learn how to read and write.

Older children study subjects such as science, geography and history. They often learn how to speak other languages too.

AT HOME

Most people who live in the Netherlands live in towns and cities. There are many different types of home that people live in, including houseboats.

HOUSEBOAT

There are also many people in the Netherlands that live and work on farms. They grow vegetables, fruit and flowers.

FAMILIES

Children usually live with their parents and their **siblings** at home. They can also live with other family members, such as their grandparents.

Dutch families like to get together to celebrate specials occasions such as weddings and birthdays.

SPORT

Football is one of the most popular sports in the Netherlands. Many people go to watch their favourite football team play.

Speed skating is also a very popular sport in the Netherlands. Children often learn how to skate at an early age.

FUN FACTS

The Netherlands is home to one of the largest flower gardens in the world. It is called Keukenhof and it is made up of over 7 million flowers.

There are over 18 million bikes in the Neatherlands, which means that there are more bikes than people!

GLOSSARY

canals	man-made waterways
Dutch	the main language spoken in the Netherlands
population	the number of people living in a place
religion	the belief in and worship of a god or gods
siblings	brothers and sisters
traditional	ways of behaving that have been done for a long time
worship	a religious act such as praying

INDEX

Photocredits: Abbreviations: l-left, r-right, b-bottom, t-top, c-centre, m-middle.
Front Cover - Sergiy Bykhunenko, bg - Aleksey Klints. 1 - Aleksey Klints. 21– MarinaDa. 3 - Sergiy Bykhunenko. 5 - Brian Kinney. 6 – symbiot. 7 – S.Borisov. 8 – FamVeld. 9 - Dennis van de Water. 10 - Eric Gevaert. 11 - Zurijeta. 12 - Elena Zajchikova. 13 – Dev_Marya. 14 - Syda Productions. 15 - wkstock. 16 - Sara Winter. 17 – MarinaDa. 18 - Max Topchii. 19 – FamVeld. 20 – Littlekidmoment. 21– YanLev. 22 - Everett – Art. 23 - Andrekart Photography. Images are courtesy of Shutterstock.com, unless stated otherwise. With thanks to Getty Images, Thinkstock Photo and iStockphoto.